The Importance of
Being an Active Citizen

Anne Beier

rosen central
Primary Source ™

Published in 2004 by The Rosen Publishing Group, Inc.
29 East 21st Street, New York, NY 10010

Library of Congress Cataloging-in-Publication Data

Beier, Anne.
The importance of being an active citizen/Anne Beier.
    p. cm.—(A Primary Source Library of American Citizenship)
Summary: Presents a guide to the responsibilities of citizenship as described in the Constitution, as well as a discussion of voting, jury duty, and military service.
Includes bibliographical references and index.
ISBN 0-8239-4475-1 (library binding)
1. Citizenship—United States—Juvenile literature. 2. Civics—Juvenile literature. [1. Citizenship. 2. Civics.]
I. Title. II. Series.
JK1759.B36 2004
323.6'5'0973—dc21

2003007178

Manufactured in the United States of America

On the cover: Top right: African Americans sit on a jury for the first time, shortly after ratification of the Fourteenth Amendment in 1868. Bottom left: On November 7, 2000, voters in New York City cast their ballots in the presidential election. Background: The text of the Nineteenth Amendment to the Constitution, granting women the right to vote, ratified in 1920.

Photo credits: cover (background) © Ratified Amendments, 1795 to 1992, general records of the United States Government, Record Group 11, National Archives and Records Administration; cover (top right), pp. 9, 17, 22, 25 © Bettmann/Corbis; cover (bottom left) © Erik Freeland/Corbis Saba; p. 5 © Record Group II, general records of the United States Government, Old Military and Civil Records, National Archives and Records Administration; pp. 6, 27, 28 © Corbis; pp. 7, 13, 21 (bottom) © Library of Congress, Prints and Photographs Division; p. 8 © Dean Wong/Corbis; pp. 10, 12, 18, 19, 29, 30 © AP/Wide World Photos; p. 11 © Alex Wong/Getty Images; p. 15 © Hulton/ Archive/Getty Images; p. 16 © James Leynse/Corbis SABA; p. 21 (top) © Jose Luis Pelaez, Inc./ Corbis; p. 23 © AFP/Corbis; p. 24 © Jeff Cadge/Image Bank/Getty Images; p. 26 courtesy of the Defense Visual Information Center; pp. 27–28 © Corbis.

Designer: Tahara Hasan; Photo Researcher: Peter Tomlinson

Contents

1 Citizenship Equals Freedom

American citizenship is based on the United States Constitution. It gives citizens freedom and equality before the law. Citizens have responsibilities as well as rights. Some responsibilities are required by law, and others are not. Everyone must obey the law even if they disagree with it. We follow laws for the common good and to keep an orderly society.

Our Fundamental Law

The U.S. Constitution was signed on September 17, 1787. Since then there have been twenty-seven amendments (or additions) to the Constitution.

A handwritten draft of the United States Constitution, the fundamental law of the nation, from 1787. It specifies the rights and responsibilities of all citizens.

There are many forms of government. America is a democracy. All citizens are treated equally in a democracy. Everyone has the right to a free education. Education teaches us to make intelligent decisions about how we are governed. In this way, we can help change laws to keep up with current issues.

Education is essential to a democracy. Citizens must understand the laws if they are to exercise their rights responsibly and decide how they want to be governed.

The torch of liberty, from the Statue of Liberty, has become a symbol of democracy recognized all around the world.

You are a citizen if you were born in America. If one of your parents is a citizen, then you are, too. You can also become a citizen by going through the naturalization process. The naturalization process requires noncitizens to get a green card, a permit to legally reside and work in the United States, from the American government. Then they must live in America for five years. When the process is finished, an oath is taken. A person pledges to be a loyal citizen of America.

Five-year-old Ronald Keodoungsy celebrates his mother's naturalization ceremony after her immigration from Laos in 1993.

A mass naturalization ceremony held in Ebbets Field, Brooklyn, New York, in 1954. Seven thousand men and women from all over the world became American citizens.

Good citizenship does not start or end at a certain age. Everyone can become involved in different ways. Following the news helps everyone form ideas about world, national, and local issues. Active citizens take part in their community. Citizenship starts with knowing right from wrong. A good citizen will do the right thing.

Citizens should stay informed about world events. Here a Massachusetts woman reads about the 2003 war in Iraq while going to work on the subway.

Volunteering to help others is an important part of citizenship. Here President George W. Bush helps out during a food collection drive in Washington, D.C.

2 Voting Your Voice

A citizen is given the right to vote at age eighteen. Before you vote, you must register. Election Day always falls on the first Tuesday in November. Voting in elections gives a citizen a voice to help change the leaders and the laws in America.

Employees of the Board of Elections help to register voters in Chicago's City Hall. Voting is the most important way that a citizen participates in the governing of the nation.

This poster urged people to vote in the 1962 congressional elections. The elephant and the donkey are symbols of our two major political parties, the Republicans and the Democrats.

Before Election Day, it is important to consider information about the candidates running for election. When voting, a citizen will make a decision about who his or her leaders will be. Every voter gets one vote. You have a right to keep your vote a secret. In a democratic election, the majority wins.

Trial by Fire

Abraham Lincoln's second election to the presidency in 1864 occurred in the middle of the Civil War, an extraordinary example of the strength of our democracy.

The debates between Abraham Lincoln and Stephen Douglas, candidates for the presidency in the election of 1860, focused on the issue of slavery. Lincoln won, the South left the Union, and the nation faced the greatest crisis of its history.

Our political system is made up of groups called parties. The two main parties are the Republican Party and Democratic Party. Voters do not have to belong to a party. But to vote in a primary election, voters must choose a party when they register. Voters generally support a party that represents their beliefs. But they can choose to vote for a candidate in another party.

This sign identifies a polling station, a place where citizens come to cast their votes. No political campaigning is permitted near the polling stations.

The cartoonist Thomas Nast created the elephant and donkey symbols for the Republican and Democratic Parties. Here, in an 1874 cartoon, Nast attacked candidate Ulysses Grant, portraying the elephant as bloated and clumsy.

National elections choose the president, senators, and congressional representatives. All three run the national government. State elections choose the governor and state representatives. They govern matters within their state. Local elections choose the mayor and officials for towns.

Senator Hillary Rodham Clinton campaigns for the New Jersey Democratic candidate for governor, Jim McGreevy, in 1997.

Willie Brown, 1995 candidate for mayor of San Francisco, shakes hands with supporters two days before the election.

3 Jury Duty Equals Justice

Every government has a set of laws that defines right and wrong. Americans have a right to be judged by a jury of their peers, that is, by people of similar backgrounds. The law states that citizens must appear for jury service when called. It is a duty to participate in the judicial system as a juror.

The Jury

Juries are generally made up of six or twelve jurors. Twelve jurors serve on most criminal cases. But only six jurors are required for civil disputes.

"Women are too sentimental for jury duty."
— Anti-Suffrage argument.

Above, the jury box in a courtroom. Below, a cartoon showing jurors being influenced by an emotional appeal instead of the facts.

The American symbol for justice is a blindfolded woman holding a balance (a scale). The idea is that justice works only when the facts are weighed and the judge is impartial. As a trial begins, the judge directs the jury to listen only to the facts. It is a juror's duty to ignore prejudice and hold a defendant innocent until proven otherwise.

To show impartiality, the figure of justice is usually depicted wearing a blindfold, as in this eighteenth-century woodcut.

Judge Nikki Clark listens to lawyers' arguments in a Tallahassee, Florida, courtroom in 2000. She was called to decide on the validity of absentee ballots in the Bush-Gore presidential election campaign.

Imagine if you were on trial. Lawyers represent all those involved. Everyone would want the jurors and the judge to be impartial. It is one of the most important duties of a citizen to keep the trial fair.

A judge calls lawyers to his bench to discuss a point of law out of the hearing of jurors so that they won't be improperly influenced.

A newspaper illustration drawn some time after the Civil War (1861–1865) shows African Americans serving on juries with whites for the first time.

4 Military Service

The armed forces exist to protect America and our freedom. The four major armed forces are the army, navy, air force, and marines. Citizens can choose a career in the military. The armed services need many people with skills besides soldiering. They need computer technicians, doctors, nurses, and lawyers, to name a few.

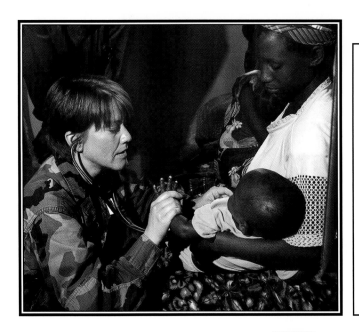

Captain Lee Ranstrom of the United States Air Force examines a sick child in Nampula, Mozambique. The armed forces often act as foreign ambassadors, providing basic life support, disaster management, and exposure to American culture.

This is the famous recruiting poster of Uncle Sam created by James Montgomery Flagg in 1917 during World War I.

When male American citizens turn eighteen, they must register for the draft. Today, we have an all-volunteer army. But in an emergency, the government may draft citizens to serve in the armed forces without their consent.

Blindfolded, Secretary of War Newton D. Baker draws draft numbers from a bowl in 1918. Those whose numbers were selected were drafted into the armed services.

Secretary of War Henry Stimson draws draft numbers in 1940 as President Franklin D. Roosevelt looks on. The nation was not yet at war, but would be the following year.

The military defends the nation as a whole. It cannot act as a local police force, except if the government declares martial law and suspends citizens' rights. That has happened on occasion, but it is a very big step to take. Usually, the units of soldiers used are from the National Guard. The National Guard is controlled by the states, not by the federal government.

Members of the Virginia National Guard stand at attention in 2002. These soldiers served for six months in Afghanistan in the war against terrorism.

Glossary

candidate (KAN-dih-dayt) Someone who is running for an election.
draft (DRAFT) The selection of people to serve in the armed forces.
impartial (im-PAR-shuhl) Being fair and not favoring one person or point of view over another.
issue (IH-shoo) The main topic for debate or decision.
loyal (LOY-uhl) Faithful to a person or idea.
majority (muh-JOR-ih-tee) More than half of a group of people.
naturalize (NA-chuh-ruhl-ize) To give citizenship to someone who was born in another country.
oath (OHTH) A serious or formal promise.
register (REH-jih-stur) To enter something on an official list.
volunteer (vah-lun-TEER) To offer to do a job, usually without pay.

Web Sites

Due to the changing nature of Internet links, the Rosen Publishing Group, Inc., has developed an online list of Web sites related to the subject of this book. This site is updated regularly. Please use this link to access the list:

http://www.rosenlinks.com/pslac/ibac

Primary Source Image List

Page 5: The United States Constitution, 1787.
Page 6: Girl reading in front of class, photographed by Larry Williams, 2002.
Page 7: Poster, "Democracy . . . a challenge," from the Illinois Works Progress Administration, created sometime between 1936 and 1940.
Page 8: *Happy Citizenship Mom!* Photographed by Dean Wong, Seattle, Washington, 1993.
Page 9: Ebbets Field ceremony, Brooklyn, New York, 1954.
Page 10: A woman on subway, photographed by Josh Reynolds, 2003.
Page 11: George W. Bush visits Washington, DC, area food bank, photographed by Alex Wong, 2002.
Page 12: Chicago Board of Elections, photographed by Brandi Wade Thomas, 2002.
Page 13: Cartoon by Bruce Alexander Russell, published in the *Los Angeles Times*, 1962.

Page 16: Polling station, New York City, photographed by James Leynse, 1996.
Page 17: Republican elephant, drawn by Thomas Nast, 1874.
Page 18: Hillary Clinton and Jim McGreevy, photographed by Mike Derer for AP, 1997.
Page 19: Willie Brown, photographed by Lacy Atkins for AP, 1995.
Page 21 (top): Jury box, photographed by Jose Pelaez, 2001.
Page 21 (bottom): Cartoon by Chamberlain, 1915, now housed at the Library of Congress.
Page 22: *Justice*, woodcut, eighteenth century.
Page 23: Judge Nikki Clark, photographed by Tim Sloan, 2000.
Page 27: *I Want You for the U.S. Army*, by James Montgomery Flagg, 1917.
Page 28: Drawing draft numbers, June 1918.
Page 30: Virginia National Guard, photographed by P. Kevin Morley for the *Richmond Times Dispatch*, 2002.

Index

About the Author

Anne Beier is a freelance writer who lives in Ossining, New York.